NEVER GIVE UP ON LOVE

NEVER GIVE UP ON LOVE

PAMELA CECILLA SMITH

J. Merrill
PUBLISHING

ISBN: 978-1-950719-52-5 (Paperback)
ISBN: 978-1-950719-51-8 (eBook)

Library of Congress Control Number: 2020917720

J Merrill Publishing, Inc.
434 Hillpine Drive
Columbus, OH 43207

www.JMerrillPublishingInc.com

I dedicate this book to my husband, Jack, and my children, Melissa, Moncherie, Jacqueline, Jack Jr., and Jermaine.

CONTENTS

FOREWORD

From Melissa Farris:

If there were pictures in the Bible depicting the characters, my mother would be captioned as the Proverbs 31 Woman. She is the epitome of this woman in every way. She is and has always been, a woman of prayer and an example of excellence in everything she put her hands to.

God truly showed my sister and I favor, when he blessed us with our mother. The foundation He placed us on as children was priceless, and I wouldn't trade the love and happiness that we shared for anything. To discuss in detail the experiences that we have had with this woman of God, would take another book.

I often reflect on the days of my youth and being with my mother, as she has been there for us through every transition of life - the good, the bad, and the ugly. I am so blessed and thankful to call her both mother *and* friend. I am so proud to see her walking through another beautiful transition of her own.

God has placed you here, Ms. Pam, (as so many friends have called you) as a beacon of light in the darkness. You have been that light for my sister, myself, and many others through the years. Every day, I thank God for you and the miracle of your life. I am so excited to witness the plans that God has purposed for this new season of life.

Congratulations on your new adventure, my Angel.

∼

From Moncherie Chapman:

Kudos to Pamela C. Smith! My Mother! "The" modern-day, Proverbs 31 Wife and Mother on her first book! This virtuous woman is truly valued far above rubies! She does her husband good and not evil all the days of her life, and her children do indeed call her blessed! My mother has exemplified love, strength, honor, compassion, and courage throughout her life.

She taught us to love, have integrity, be a woman of our word, and show empathy as we are all only one mistake or sin away from failure. She also taught us humility. We know that every good thing comes from God, and we are nothing without Him. And, when we strayed, she was right there to remind us of who and whose we were.

My mother was and is a Prayer Warrior. She was always my first call when there was a need to be lifted to the Father or to acknowledge and celebrate His graciousness in answering prayer. I have been the recipient of healings and miracles that I know resulted from her constant prayer over my life.

My sister and I were raised to have a servant's heart. We worked alongside her, cleaning the homes of elderly church and community members, running errands, and taking food to those in need. I watched my parents dedicate their lives to God's kingdom. They worked tirelessly in the church, hosting a radio ministry, and growing an intercessory prayer ministry that impacted many lives.

Being one that never tires of growing in God, Mom went back to college in her 60s. She took religious studies courses to deepen her knowledge and understanding of God's word. My mother's story is proof of God's agape love for us. For as she walked in love and obedience to God throughout her life, He never forgot her young heart's first love. I believe He needed her services, but as only God in his omniscience can, He knew the end of the story that she is about to share with you.

I pray you are as blessed by her sharing of her life as I was by living it as her daughter.

MY HEART'S DESIRE: AN INTRODUCTION

"DELIGHT THYSELF IN THE LORD, AND HE WILL GIVE THEE THE DESIRES OF THINE HEART." PSALM 37:4

My heart's desire as a young girl was to marry in white, as this pure color was a testament to all in attendance that the bride was a virtuous young lady. I was a dreamer with quite a vivid imagination. So I spent many quiet moments dreaming about my future husband, our life together, and the children we might have one day.

When I did meet my first love as a young teen, we were only together for a short time before our lives took us away from each other for the next fifty-two years. But even in our separate lives, we had similar experiences with both divorces and losing a spouse to cancer. After decades apart and a time of healing, God saw fit to breathe life into that long-forgotten love from the past.

I was in Texas in 2008, visiting family two years after the death of my precious husband Jim, when I had a vivid dream about a certain young man I knew in my youth. The dream was very odd at the time as I had not seen or heard from him in many, many years. But, as I stated before, God knows the desires of our hearts... and his memory does not fade. I am writing this book to encourage all women that, with God's help, it is never too late for love.

MY CHILDHOOD

"TRAIN UP A CHILD IN THE WAY HE SHOULD GO;
AND WHEN HE IS OLD, HE WILL NOT DEPART FROM
IT." PROVERBS 22:6

N ow, I would like to tell you a little about my life as a young girl. My "back-story," so to say, began in the household of Elder Willie and Evangelist Cassie Grant of Wyoming county, WV. I was raised in a family of seven children and was the third of six children born to Cassie and Willie. My oldest brother was Willie Jr., my oldest sister was Thelma, I was in the middle, then Danny, Carol (Pinky), and Sammy. He was our mother's heart and image. "Little Pam" joined our family when I was 15 or 16. She was adopted within the family, which was common back then. People rarely turned to the outside for help. Family and neighbors stepped up and took care of one another.

Wyoming County was in the heart of the WV mountains and was best known for its abundant coal fields. We lived in Black Eagle and Corrine, both outside of Mullens, WV. As children, we played in the Coal Tipple, which was used to dump the coal collected from the mines into the large open top railroad cars that hauled it away. To the children of our day, it resembled a large metal slide. After the men had stopped work, most of the kids in the neighborhood would go the tipple to play. The tipple was never cleaned, so when we returned home, we were filthy, entirely covered in black coal dust. Naturally, our parents would have a fit, but that is what we loved to do. For me, playing in the tipple made us all the same. See, I was born with a very fair complexion, as was my baby brother. But unlike today, this was not a positive attribute in a coal mining town. I was often teased as I did not look like the other black children. Until we played in the tipple, then no one could really tell much of a difference.

I was raised in a very strict Christian home, where I was not allowed to do much outside of Church and School. However, I can remember an exception being made when a very special someone asked my mother if I could go to the movies. She pondered this outing for some time.

She finally agreed, but only if we took my younger sister, Pinky. I was surprised at my mother's approval as movies were considered a "sin" in those days. We were also not allowed to attend dances or visit local juke joints. Even listening to soul music, later called "secular" music, was heavily frowned upon. We were, however, allowed to watch American Bandstand when it finally reached us in WV. But we were not allowed to dance along.

We were also not allowed to visit surrounding neighborhoods or coal camps without permission and adult supervision. The coal camps were often segregated. So, one would be mostly black, while another white. We didn't totally understand this growing up, so it felt that our world was very small.

My brothers were allowed much more freedom and were very creative. I do not ever remember anyone using the word "bored." Old broken down cars were littered all around our coal camp. My brothers, who were all gifted in different ways, would take the roofs off of these old cars, do some limited repairs with whatever tools that they might have on hand, and voila! They had a boat! They would actually put it in the river, and off they would go in their new boat.

My brothers were also allowed to go swimming, but my sisters and I could not, as my mother feared what might happen to the girls swimming on their own. Our parents could not take us to a pool, as we did not have one in the black coal camp, and it was understood that blacks were not allowed in the public pool or library in Mullens. The boys, however, swam in various spots in the river. It was years later that we realized that both were polluted due to the nearby mining, but God kept them safe. The boys enjoyed all of the rough and tough stuff offered in our mountainous environment, but not the girls.

The Glorious Church of God had a baptism service on the creek bank in Corrine, which was a big event for my small town. I accepted Jesus as my Lord and Savior and was baptized in His name at the age of nine. As I was going in the water, I overheard a woman say, "That child does not know what she is doing. She is too young." When I came out of the water, I did something that children in that day did not, because it was considered rude or sassy. I told her that I loved Jesus just as she did, and I did know what I was doing. This day marked a turning point in my life. I saw people receiving the Holy Spirit (scripture), and I wanted it. I was more aware of my actions and my spiritual connection with my Savior. Though still very young, I was determined to live a Godly life.

As a young spirit-filled Christian of my day, sometimes life was not easy. We were not as popular as other religious groups. Our strict rules and required attire made it easy to distinguish us from other young people our age. In addition to movies and dancing, we were also not allowed to "date," wear pants, jewelry, make-up, or any kind of "adornment." The sacrifices required did not really bother me because I loved God. Our lives were still full of joy and happiness because of the relationship we had with our parents, our tight-knit community, and the other holy children like us. This helped us to live the life that God required.

When young people gave their lives to God, they were faithful in being true to the Lord.

I loved the Lord so much that I would go to church with anyone that asked. I was always ready to spend more time with God. I remember going to church with my friend, Barbara Robinson, and her father, Rev. Felix Robinson. He pastored a church in Sun, WV, which was a one hour drive each way from where we lived. He held services two Sundays each month, and I loved to attend and hear him preach.

I also enjoyed hearing my Uncle, Bishop John Grant, minister God's word. At that time, my uncle was not a bishop. He was ordained a bishop two years before his death, which was a great and worthy honor, as he was a wonderful man of God.

As children, my parents took us to several churches. In that day, you had no voice in anything, especially concerning the church. As I look back, I learned so much about the different denominations. I realized that the separation of the denominational churches prevented us from being in fellowship with all of God's children. There were precious men and women of God that never had the opportunity to fellowship with one another, which is so sad. I have always felt that if you loved Jesus, you should have been able to love your brothers and sisters, even if they were not in your denomination. I have learned so much through the years concerning our love for one another in the body of Christ.

My parents often attended a church in Raven Cliffe, WV, The Church of God of Prophecy, where the late Reverend Duty was the pastor. Before our attendance, the church congregation was all white. From my memory, we were the only black family to ever attend. As a child, you had to obey your parents in all things, and that included your church life. So, we adapted very quickly and fell in love with everyone, especially the children. My sister and I went to the church's summer youth camp in Culloden, West Virginia, for several years. It was quite a trip for us as we rarely traveled for long distances. The drive to Culloden was three to four hours as it was northwest of us, between Charleston, the state capital, and Huntington, one of the larger cities in WV. We stayed for a week, and it was always a great time. We attended the summer camp the year I turned twelve. I will never forget that summer as I received my personal gift from God, the Holy Spirit. Oh, what a time our young people's group experienced. Serving God was so exciting, we could not wait until our evening youth services!

Our family fell in love with the Tolliver family. They attended The Church of God of Prophecy, and they also had several children. Their mother was an excellent cook, and we enjoyed the Sunday meals we had at their home after church. The Tolliver's had a daughter named Bonnie, that was my age. One of the highlights of my youth was being invited to spend the weekend on their farm. I had never been on a farm. So, I was really excited. I never thought about skin color. But I saw my mother's hesitancy. I realized she was concerned for my safety going into an all-white neighborhood alone. But as was customary for my mother, she prayed about it and put me in the Lord's hands, and I could go. I was so excited about the animals, but I also loved the farm part of it. I loved fresh fruit and vegetables, and they had all kinds of fruit trees. I also rode a horse and was able to watch Mrs. Tolliver make butter and creamed corn. The food was so fresh and delicious, it was truly heavenly. I never forgot Mrs. Tolliver's cream corn and chicken and dumpling recipe. They are both now my family favorites, requested by my daughters whenever we are together.

We had an old dirt road with no signage, but everyone knew it was Tram Rd. It went on for miles twisting and turning straight up into the West Virginia mountains. About halfway to our destination, we would pass a small house where the Sizemore's lived. They had the only house on the mountain, and they were a very lovely white family that were friends of my parents. They also had several children, so they would join us for the rest of the trek up the mountain. This was a fun trip for me and my siblings despite the long walk as mother always sent us together, me, my older sister, and the two older brothers. Pinky and Sammy were still too small for such a long walk. Our destination? The apple orchards! They had an old fashioned apple orchard with beautiful apples that we were allowed to pick. They never asked for payment, and we would often pick so many that my sister and I would take off our dresses. Because we wore whole slips under our dresses, we were able to do this and still be modestly covered. Our dresses became our sacks. When we came home wearing our slips, with our dresses full of apples, our parents had no reason to worry. They knew our intentions were pure, and there was nothing evil afoot, as we just wanted to get as many apples home as possible. You must remember, we lived in a coal camp in the 1940s-1960s, and there was no grocery store close by. Though we never went hungry, free, fresh apples turned into fried apples for breakfast and apple pie for Sunday dinner, which were treats for the entire family.

~

I WENT to two all-black schools, Conley Grade School for grades 1-6, was in Goose Hollow near Mullens, WV, and Conley High School for grades 7-12 was in Caloric, Wyoming County, also near Mullens. I did not see this as negative, as all my teachers were members of our community. And knew they were responsible for preparing us for life and took their role very seriously. They saw to it that we all received an excellent education. At school, my teachers were like my mother and father. If a child came to school dirty or smelly, the teachers were always prepared, as the adage goes, "Johnny on the spot." They always had a toothbrush and toothpaste, or soap and washcloth. A black teacher back in the day was worth their weight in gold to the community and its students. If they spanked your butt at school for misbehaving or being unprepared, there was no call needed. You went home and told your mother what you did and received your second spanking as they felt you deserved it for not doing right in school.

I can only remember one school-related instance in which my mother knew something was not right and challenged one of my teachers. I believe

I was in the sixth grade, and as stated earlier, I had a lighter complexion. I came home from school that day with a big red mark on the side of my face, and I think it was a little puffy. I can remember Mom looking at my face and asking me what happened. I told her my teacher "smacked me," and that she smacked all the kids. I loved learning and was not a headstrong or sassy child, so this was not a normal situation for me. Oh, but my mother! She went to the school, and it was on! I was fearful and happy at the same time. Glad that my mother was defending me and the other kids, but also afraid of my teacher's possible backlash. But, Ms. Cassie (my mom) was in control. There was no yelling or threatening. My mother simply had a conversation. She explained that I was her child, and she would not tolerate anyone putting their hands on my face again. That was it. I never had another issue.

I graduated in 1965, which was the beginning of the desegregation of schools in WV. My younger siblings then attended integrated schools, and the community based, safe education I experienced was lost to them. For the most part, they still flourished despite the hardships they encountered. One situation that I never understood was when we moved into Black Eagle,

WV. We were not allowed to catch the bus in front of our house like the white children that lived across the street. We had to walk about a mile on a dirt road in the opposite direction, even when there was another closer bus stop just a stone throw down the hill from our house.

What would I change about my childhood? Nothing! I enjoyed my childhood, my family, friends, and Godly upbringing all made me who I am today.

2

MY DADDY

"HEARKEN UNTO THY FATHER THAT BEGAT THEE,
AND DESPISE NOT THY MOTHER WHEN SHE IS
OLD." PROVERBS 23:22

My father, Willie Grant, Sr. was a coal miner. He was from a large family in Raleigh County, WV. He migrated to coal camps of Wyoming County like so many men at that time, looking for work to support their families. He was a hard worker and very well respected in our coal camp. He would leave for work before dawn and come back by early evening. As a child, we did not pay attention to time, but I suspect he worked 8-10 hours a day. When he got home, he went straight into his prized garden. It was not your typical small family garden; it was more of a farm. It was so large that it required that he work almost every evening until dark. So, it was rare for us to have daily contact with our father because he was always working. When he finally came in from the garden, we were going to bed. He grew green beans, corn, potatoes, tomatoes, squash, sweet potatoes, and various greens, along with some fruits. He was the only one in our coal camp that could grow melons, and he was very proud of this. You name it, he could grow it. My father honestly had a green thumb. We did not have to go to the grocery store for vegetables, which was a savings and a blessing for our large family. We only went to the store for bread, meat, and some fruits that Daddy couldn't grow in the WV climate.

Daddy's garden was across the river from where we lived, and I believe he rented the land from a local neighbor. He was rarely hindered once he got an idea related to his garden. He knew the ground next to the river was fertile as it flooded every few years, which made the soil rich for planting. He decided to build a swinging bridge for easier daily access. He made the swinging bridge with cable and scrap wood, and it worked just as he knew it would. He had no internet or written directions, only his memory, imagination, and the meager materials from the coal camp or the local supply store, which was limited. My dad was always doing different things to help our family and community.

When he heard that a nearby coal camp had clear television reception, which was hard to get in our area nestled in a valley with mountains all around, he started working on a solution. One day Daddy climbed high into the mountains with his very own homemade antenna. When he came back, the entire camp had better television reception, and everyone was so grateful.

My daddy was a very smart man. He did not finish high school as he went to work to help his family, as was customary in the day. But while he did not have "book smarts," he was a natural builder and creator, which now would be considered an engineer, I guess. He did things that our neighbors could not believe. He soon was given the nickname "Do Right," as he was always doing the right thing in both the mines and for our community. Back then, people just did not have the knowledge or access to books, etc. to do the things he did. He did not just dream. If he saw a need, he would make a plan, start gathering his materials and do it! He was really something!

We lived in a typical coal camp house that only had four rooms: a kitchen, living area, and two bedrooms, with no bathroom. In our coal camp, everyone still used outhouses, but as our family grew, so did our house. By the time Dad was done, we had an eight-room house. The girls and boys had their own bedroom, he expanded the kitchen to allow for a bigger dining area. We were one of the first homes in the camp to have a full inside bathroom, and Dad did all the plumbing and construction himself. Dad truly had a gift. All he needed to do was see something done, and he could do it. He never called an electrician, plumber, or a handyman. He could figure out anything and just get it done.

My Parents took in an older woman who had been widowed named Nanny Cecil. My parents married very young. Sis. Cecil, as she was called in Church circles, was a great help to my mother when she had 3 children in 6 years and was only 21 years old. My mother had delivered all 6 of her children by the time she was 27, which was not uncommon in that day. My middle name was an error by the hospital derived from Cecil but spelled on my birth certificate as "Cecilla." Sis. Cecil's arrival put Daddy back to work, and we gained a fourth bedroom. She lived with us during a period when the coal miners went on strike for better pay and conditions. My mom went to New York to work with the other younger women in the community. She was blessed as she was able to do work that she was accustomed to. She became a Nanny, taking care of the children and home of a wealthy Jewish family. She would send money to help sustain the household during the strike. I am not sure how long Mom was gone, but I suspect it was less than 1 year. I remember one Christmas, she sent my older sister and I a beautiful charm bracelet with a heart on it. My sister and I were in awe of such a beautiful gift! As children, we did not have jewelry, and our Parents rarely wore more than their wedding bands. In our minds, the bracelets were priceless, so rare and precious, we truly cherished them, though they were probably quite inexpensive. That bracelet was all we received for Christmas, and we were happy.

3

THE PIANO

"MAKE A JOYFUL NOISE UNTO THE LORD, ALL THE
EARTH; MAKE A LOUD NOISE, AND REJOICE, AND
SING PRAISE." PSALMS 98:4

Aunt Rebecca was a very blessed lady. My uncle loved her dearly and spoiled her with her every heart's desire. She was the first person I knew to own a baby grand piano. I believe that my dad felt that if Uncle JC could buy a piano for his family, then our family should have one as well. So, when I was twelve, my daddy bought "me" a piano, hoping that I would be the musician in the family. I will never forget when the shiny black up-right Wurlitzer arrived. It was quite a prize for a family as in our coal camp, only the occasional church had a piano. They were very rare to have in a black home.

My mother introduced me to her friend's son, who played the piano, and he agreed to give me lessons.

This young man was also from a Christian family but did not live in our coal camp. His family was from Itmann, WV. He was a few years older, so I had rarely encountered him. His oldest sister Shelby also played the piano, and his youngest sister Elsa sang with him and their mother. They had a very musically gifted family and were respected in the community.

I continued my lessons on the piano until I turned thirteen and went into junior high school. I am not sure exactly when, but I started seeing my piano teacher in a different light. He was an upperclassman, and suddenly I was aware that he was quite handsome. Needless to say, when he was around, it became increasingly difficult to focus on my piano lessons. After one of my unproductive lessons, he asked my mother if he could take me to a movie. As stated earlier, she was very hesitant due to my age and the fact that they did not condone movies because they were thought to be "worldly." She only agreed because the movie was age-appropriate, and I had to take my baby sister (Pinky) with us as our chaperone. I never forgot my first date. The name of the theater was The Rialto. I think it cost 50 cents per ticket, and the blacks had to sit in the balcony of the theater as only the whites could sit on the main floor. I have very little memory of the actual movie as I was far too busy looking at Jack!

My oldest brother, Willie, Jr., was allowed to go to the movies when he got older. We never questioned our parents. But I can see now that there was always a double standard active in our home that benefitted the boys, but we did not really mind. Willie Jr.'s nickname was Buddha because, as a baby, he had a large round tummy. He was an awesome storyteller. Whenever he saw a new movie, he would come back home and gather all five of us around him and tell us about the movie. We'd all be sitting there with our mouths open as he described every detail of what he saw. My favorite was Tarzan. I could see the jungle and hear the sounds! We all loved these times with our brother. It was as if we were seeing through his eyes. It was amazing!

As for the piano? If any of you remember the old western, 'Have Gun, Will Travel,' this describes our piano. I practiced for about two years, but I was not very consistent. Then my brother Danny started playing. He did not take lessons, but what started out as playing around quickly turned into chords and songs. In a very short time, Danny, who we called Busta, could play anything he heard. He was musically inclined and "played by ear," as the old folk said. When Danny lost interest in his teens, the piano was loaned to several churches in the area. It traveled for two decades before it finally came back home to me.

People back in the day did not mind sharing. Material things just did not mean as much to people as they do know. That piano was probably one of the most expensive items my parents owned other than their home and vehicles. Daddy didn't care. If anyone asked, he would quickly reply, "Yeah, we'll bring it to you!"

The Grant family piano is sitting right now in a storage unit. When I moved, the piano was left in my home and was later moved into storage. When it first came back to me 40 years ago, I had it tuned and began lessons again, but my heart was no longer in it. I accepted that my brother was the musical talent in our family and admitted that it just did not come as easily to me. My children even took lessons and played the piano for a time. I am sure the piano has reached the end of its life, far exceeding the 5 years I was told it had left over 20 years ago. I have given my sister permission to pass it on or trash it. For years, the piano reminded me of a person and period of my life that made me smile, sadly for what I thought was lost. But I no longer need a memento. I can let the piano go knowing that it served the family and all that used it very well.

4

LIFE AFTER GRADUATION

"THE STEPS OF A GOOD MAN ARE ORDERED BY THE LORD; AND HE DELIGHTETH IN HIS WAY." PSALM 37:23

I graduated from Conley High School in May of 1965. My mother bought me red Samsonite luggage as my graduation gift, and it was packed and ready for my move to Jersey City, NJ, the next day. My cousin's husband worked at a collection agency and had already lined up a job for me. I interviewed on Monday and went to work on Tuesday. I worked directly with Lawyer Greenberg and Edith Tully, his office manager, for a little over a year before I went to work in New York at Chase Manhattan Bank. I lived in New Jersey for ten years and met some beautiful people.

I loved my job and my co-workers. I learned so much from Lawyer Greenburg and Ms. Tully.

They understood I was a country girl with no exposure. They appreciated my work ethic and sincere desire to do a good job. They helped me daily with my speech, pronunciation, and vocabulary. Being from the country, I had a deep West Virginia drawl. Though I graduated Salutatorian in my class, I did not "sound" like it. Before long, I was speaking more clearly and quickly and using a few of the legal terms and phrases that were necessary for my position. They also helped me understand and navigate city life. There were so many people, and everyone moved so fast! I had to learn quickly or be a constant target for teasing and criticism. I never forgot the impact these beautiful people had on my life.

I had been in the city for about a year when I met a very handsome man who later became my husband. He also graduated in 1965, the year before our meeting from Ferris High School in Jersey City, NJ, and his name was Stan Brown. Two years later, we had our first daughter, Melissa. Then, after his tour in the Army, where he served in the Vietnam War, he returned home, and our second daughter, Moncherie, was born. Our girls were three years apart, and they were beautiful. Melissa was born very dainty, with a fair complexion and silky brown curls. I was always stopped on the street by strangers who wanted a closer look as she looked like a living doll. But she was also a handful as she was extremely bright and had a precocious, witty personality even as a very young child.

I had to stay on toes to keep up with my beautiful firstborn. Stan and I wanted our second child to be a boy. When Moncherie was born, in those first seconds, we thought we had our desire as she was very brown like her daddy and robust, with a nearly bald head. While we were initially disappointed, Moncherie was a very good baby and won everyone's heart with her sweet disposition. Please do not feel sorry for my Moncherie as she was the favorite of her father's family as she looked so much like them. She grew into a very confident child and a beautiful woman, as did her older sister. Our life was happy at times. Stan preferred that I not work and focus on caring for our small daughters. Life was very hard on one salary, and I wanted to return to work for myself and my family, but Stan disagreed.

One day I realized how unhappy I was. I talked to my mother about certain things that were happening in my marriage and in my life. She informed me anytime I wanted to come home, the girls and I were welcome, and she would send me money for the train. When I reached the end of my tolerance, I knew I had tried my best and endured enough. I made that fateful call to my mother.

I did not want a confrontation. So, I waited for Stan to go to work one day, and I packed one huge suitcase which contained only clothes for the girls. I was not really thinking too clearly and did not even consider myself. I believe that trip home was the worst trip of my life.

At the time, we lived in a third-floor apartment with no elevator. So you can imagine how difficult this undertaking was with a one-year-old and a four-year-old. It required that I hold Moncherie in one arm, then holding Melissa's hand, all while dragging a suitcase that was bigger than both children. Remember, we had no wheels on suitcases back then.

The Lord was with me. On arrival at the station, a nice gentleman offered to help me get to my train with the large suitcase. Back then, they also did not check your luggage. So, I had to manage the best way I could while keeping up with my little ones. But I knew once I got on the train, I would be okay as my family would be waiting for us at the train station in Prince, West Virginia.

The girls and I lived with my mom and dad at first. But to get help, I went on welfare. Back then, to receive this help, I also had to move. My brother, Sammy, took my girls and me in, which allowed us to receive assistance. I was very grateful and tried to get my life back in order as quickly as possible. I learned to drive and got my driver's license at the age of 29. I was also able to obtain a decent job to support my little family.

Based on my prior work experience with Lawyer Greenburg and Chase Manhattan Bank, I thought I would be able to quickly find work in banking. However, finding employment in West Virginia in the early 1970s was not easy. I was told that the position I held in NJ did not exist in my small town bank. This, at first, was disappointing, but it gave me the chance to change my field of work. So, I later decided to pursue something in the medical field for job security.

My first job was with Community Action out of Oceana, West Virginia. I was given a caseload of low-income families and was responsible for completing home visits to verify certain information. This was a very interesting job as a black woman.

See, most of my caseload was in the most rural areas of Wyoming County, and most of the children had never seen a black person. I worked in Barkus Ridge, Alpoca, Bud Mountain, and Stephenson. I wasn't there long as I worked alone, and it was not really safe for me at the time. I really wanted to work in Beckley, which was the largest city in the area, and only 45 minutes away from where I was living.

My desire to work in Beckley came about through my father, Willie Grant, and his friend, Robert Payne. They were working with the United Mine Workers union and a local black lung support association because they had contracted (Pneumoconiosis) Black Lung disease from working underground in the mines. They were both forced into early retirement after being awarded disability. My father was injured in a mine collapse in addition to developing black lung from 30 years mining coal underground. I still lived in Mullens but obtained my first job in Beckley, working with Doctor Donald Rasmussen. He treated my father and Mr. Payne at the Miner's Hospital.

The doctor hired me directly, but I was given no formal training and just learned on the job. A co-worker would tease me daily, stating, "Last hired, first fired." He was white and liked to remind me that I had no formal training or certification. He indirectly influenced my decision to seek additional education and the certification I needed for job security in the medical field. I was there for almost 1 year when I saw a training program advertised at the Veteran Hospital for a Clinical Laboratory Assistant. I immediately applied for the program, and Dr. Rasmussen agreed to send a reference for me. I did not know until later that entrance into the program was very competitive. Approximately fifty applied, and only six were accepted that year. Historically, only one black was allowed in each class. The year I was selected, two blacks were admitted. I later understood that it was Dr. Rasmussen's glowing reference that secured my spot in the program. I was so proud to obtain my certification as a Clinical Laboratory Assistant in December of 1975. The training program was full-time for one year, and very difficult for a single mom raising two children with a 45-minute commute each way. But I did it with many 4:00 am study sessions at the kitchen table before it was time to wake the girls and get us ready for the day. Due to the many people that applied, a similar program was created at Beckley College. It was a two-year program that offered certification as a Medical Laboratory Technician. The college classes were at least three times the cost of my program, which was ended because of the new one at the college. Let us just agree here that God is good!

I obtained my first position, in my certification, at Oak Hill Hospital, in Oak Hill, WV. I was still living in Mullens, which was over an hour's drive each way. In 1976 I finally moved to Beckley, WV. Stan came back into my life when he brought my furniture and personal belongings that I left behind in New Jersey. A few days' visit turned into a second chance. This was in part due to my religious convictions and my father's belief that once divorced, I could never re-marry. The marriage didn't last, and within months of moving to Beckley, it was finally over.

As my daughters grew, I knew they would become aware of the moral and emotional issues in the home. I never wanted to set an example that they would follow in their own lives by being a man's doormat. It also became apparent to my parents that I did indeed have biblical grounds for divorce.

When I asked Stan to leave, I asked him for nothing. I had my girls, and I knew God would make a way for me to pay for the house and take care of our expenses as he had done in the past. So much happened in the 3 short years since my return to WV. I went from being a welfare recipient to a driving, educated, single mom, and a homeowner. Through the support of my family and guidance of my heavenly Father, I made it through.

I went on to work at Beckley Hospital, Rural Acres Clinic, and Southern WV Clinic, all in Beckley. I started working in the Lab at Southern WV Clinic. I was only at that location for a few years before being offered a lab position at Dr. Carl Larson's new oncology clinic, Raleigh Regional Cancer Center on Dry Hill Rd in Beckley.

Before leaving Southern WV Clinic, I found myself being courted by a retired Air Force Master Sargent from Mt. Hope, WV. James Leonard, Jr. was a medic in the military and went on to complete his RN. He returned home to take care of his parents, who were getting older and started working at Appalachian Regional Hospital, which was right beside the Southern WV Clinic. We met when he was searching the hospital for a patient who had escaped the psychiatric ward, and I was picking up some lab specimens for work.

We married in 1978. Jim was a wonderful husband and father. He helped me raise my two daughters, who adored him, and he saw that both went to college. Jim found salvation in the early years of our marriage and became a scholar of God's word. We attended several churches in Beckley but spent the most time as a family with The Outreach for Christ Christian Center, pastored by Thomas Steelman. We ministered together, having a radio program and intercessory prayer group, and he loved to praise and worship God! Our family was very happy. He was blessed to see both girls finish college, get married, and have their own families before losing a short battle to cancer.

God was merciful as we received his diagnosis in late September. I will never forget as the girls had planned a big party for my birthday, and we wanted to cancel. However, we decided to continue as we suspected it would be the last time for him to see everyone while still doing reasonably well.

After 28 years of marriage, Jim went on to be with the Lord just two short weeks later. He told everyone that he was ready to meet his God face-to-face. He was indeed a man that pleased God.

A year after Jim's death, I went to New Jersey to visit my old friend, Leola Kennedy. We met shortly after we both graduated high school, and I moved to New Jersey. Our friendship has since spanned over fifty years.

We both tried to visit when life would allow. When I visited her after Jim's death, she wanted to lift my spirits by treating me to a cruise on the Hudson River. We both have two daughters. My oldest, Melissa, was born a year after Leola's oldest daughter, Vanessa; and Leola's youngest, Jan, was born two years after my Moncherie. Through life's changes and up and downs, Leola has always been a true friend, despite the distance. So when the time came, she was my first choice for Matron of Honor.

5
___

REUNITED

"DELIGHT THYSELF ALSO IN THE LORD AND HE
SHALL GIVE THEE THE DESIRES OF THINE HEART."
PSALM 37:4

After Jim died in 2006, I was a little lost. Having been married for most of my adult life, I needed to find direction for myself as a widow. I always loved education and wanted to go to college, so I did. I talked to a lovely lady at Beckley College, which is now Mountain State University. I explained my interest in learning more about the history of religion and the Bible.

They did not have a biblical studies program. But, she was able to recommend some classes and even explained a program they had that would allow me to develop my own course of study and classes. I took several of these classes because of my interest in the various religions and where the different denominations originated. I have always felt that we should all be serving the one true God, or the holy trinity of The Father, The Son of God, and the Holy Spirit. My studies kept me busy, and God had also given me a mission during this time. He had me visiting local churches in Beckley outside of the denominations that I knew to see for myself how they viewed and worshipped God. I learned so much and greatly enjoyed this time of exploration, which confirmed for me that these churches were also grounded in God's love. When my designated time was up, I said, "Lord, which one of these churches will you have me attend?" His answer was totally unexpected. I heard clearly, "Do not worry about a church home, you will go to church with your husband." I immediately said, "God, I have not asked you for a husband." This was in August of 2009. I had no way of knowing that God was about to do a quick work in my life that would begin with a fateful phone call just 2 months later.

As mentioned earlier, I visited my long-time girlfriend, Leola Kennedy, in New Jersey. I also made several trips to North Carolina to visit my adopted mother. My son-in-law, William, who is married to my youngest daughter, Moncherie, is blessed to still have both of his grandmother's living. While both are lovely women of God, Roberta Chapman ("Mama"), who is William's maternal grandmother, reminded me of my mother and the holy women of old that I grew up with. From our first meeting, I loved her. She was in her mid-eighties, but sharp as a tack, with a meek spirit and profound wisdom.

I lost my mother in 1997 and never knew my maternal grandmother. I never heard Mama say a negative or harsh word, and her deep love for her family was a blessing to witness. We enjoyed crocheting together and talking about God's word. Her daughters became my adopted sisters. The time I spent with Lillian, William's mother, and Lossie, his Aunt, were filled with the laughter and the banter of a loving family. I later met their 3rd sister, Vaughn, who previously lived in Utah. My trips to North Carolina provided the healing that my heart needed, and I will always love my extended family.

I would be remiss if I did not mention Mr. Chapman's (William's father) garden. See, I inherited my daddy's love of gardening, so I appreciate and admire anyone with a green thumb. I always looked forward to seeing his garden when I visited NC as it far exceeded anything I could do. It reminded me of my dad's garden across the river when I was a young girl. I always left with a bag of hand-picked fresh vegetables. Greens, corn, tomatoes, I was happy to take whatever was in season at the time of my visit.

I was on my way back from one of my visits to North Carolina when my happily ever after began. I was on the highway when my cell phone rang. I thought it was Lillian or one of my girls checking on me, but I did not recognize the number. I was pleasantly surprised to hear one of my old classmates, Alice Payne, on the line. We graduated from Conley together and saw each other a few times a year at various social or church gatherings. We only spoke briefly, and she told me she had someone with her that wanted to talk to me. Well, I instantly recognized the voice to be that of Jackie Smith. He told me he was leaving Bluefield, where he had attended his Aunt's 100th birthday and was on his way back to Ohio with his sister, Elsa, and Alice. As they had to pass through Beckley, he decided to call and see if they could attend church service with my family and me. I was momentarily speechless. I had not heard from or seen Jackie in nearly 30 years.

Our lives went in separate directions when his family moved to Columbus, OH. I remember he returned to WV and wanted to take me out just before going into the military and my graduation from High School, but both of our mothers' refused. We understood later that they were trying to save us some heartache. We saw each other only twice over the next 50 years at random church or social functions. I knew from family and friends that Jackie had married after his time in Vietnam. He also had a family of his own as I did, and that was that. I thought of him after my first marriage ended but was happy to hear that he and his wife were doing well. While I had 2 young daughters, they had 2 little sons. I did again hear through church circles that he lost his wife to cancer, and my heart went out to him, but I was happily married to my Jim, and that was that.

Back to that initial phone call: I informed Jack that I had lost my husband to cancer almost three years prior and that I was driving back from North Carolina. I told him I was enjoying traveling and was quite happy as a widow. I also told him quite clearly that I was not looking for a spouse. This was a statement that I had made many times when asked about my interest in marriage or dating. But by the then end of the conversation, I quoted a very familiar scripture to him, *"A man that findeth a wife, findeth a good thing and obtains favor of the Lord."* I found myself being a bit feisty as I was enjoying our conversation very much. I explained that any man that was interested in me would have to come to 119 Plumley Ave, where I lived since I was not looking for a man or marriage. I was so surprised to hear from him after so many years, but I also questioned God. I was not looking to date, I was not lonely, and I did not feel I needed "another" husband.

But as I talked to God, He reminded me of a conversation I had with Jim shortly before he passed. Our last trip out together was to Grandview State Park. We enjoyed the beautiful scenery, and on our drive back home, Jim told me not to worry, that I was going to have a full life with a husband to do all the things I have desired to do. He knew I loved to travel, but he did not, he said after 20 years in the military and traveling the world, he was fine at home. He did not like to eat out or attend social functions. He preferred my cooking and the peace and quiet of his home. No amount of pleading would make him change his mind. He was also a bit rough, and he knew it. He was a no-nonsense type of guy, refusing to take part in what he called "frivolous" conversation or activity. You could find him at work, in church, or at home in his garden, and he had no time or interest for anything other than the Word of God and his family. So, for him to tell me this, I realized that he knew he had *"fought the good fight and that his departure was at hand.* I still tear up when I think of the unselfish love in that conversation.

Well, I did not hear from Jack for several days and later learned that he got cold feet. His sister, Elsa, kept encouraging him to call me. Three days later, I received my second call. Jack asked if he could come to Beckley to pay me a visit and wanted to know when I might be available. To my surprise, he had taken down my address in that initial conversation and added it to his GPS. I still cannot explain all the thoughts and emotions that raced through my mind after that conversation. As a holy woman of God, I realized I was afraid to be courted. What would people think? As a sixty-two-year-old widow, was it acceptable to have a man in my home after dark? I must admit that I was an emotional mess and sought the counsel of my sister, Thelma, and my daughter, Melissa. They both encouraged me to be happy and not fearful.

By the time he arrived on my doorstep, I had a plan. My daughter, Melissa, would give us a few hours to talk, then she would come over to meet him as well, so we would be adequately chaperoned. I can still remember opening the door and seeing him for the first time again.

I was suddenly 17, and he was 20, and we were both smiling and laughing and comfortable as if a lifetime had not passed us by. Jack's hug was so comforting, but I was totally unprepared for the love I felt and the words he shared. Jack professed his love for me and asked me to marry him, stating he would not miss the opportunity again to make me his wife. I was speechless!

Melissa and her ex-husband, Dallas Cooper, decided to take Jack and I out to Glade Springs. This resort community had a golf course, country club, and restaurant. Melissa and I talked, while Jack and Dallas played pool. We had such a beautiful day together. I felt in my spirit that it would be the first of many.

6

ENGAGEMENT & WEDDING

"WHAT THEREFORE GOD HATH JOINED TOGETHER,
LET NO MAN PUT ASUNDER." MARK 10:9

The holidays were approaching, and I would get a chance to meet Jack's children, Jacqueline, Jack Jr., and Jermaine. I was excited to meet them, but also anxious, as you can imagine, as I was unsure of the reception I would receive. But as the good Lord says, "*Be anxious for nothing.*" All went well. His children and friends were so nice and welcoming, and I enjoyed myself very much.

After our Thanksgiving dinner, we all went bowling. This was something I had not done in many years. I enjoyed the laughter and joy that I now know is typical of his family whenever they are together.

After that trip to Columbus, things started moving quickly. Jack had met Melissa as she was living in Beckley at the time, but Moncherie was in TX. So, we planned a phone call for Jack to meet my youngest. She was a bit more skeptical as she feared me being hurt again after the death of her father. But it was not long before she saw my happiness, and Jack's love for me was real.

My greatest joy was to see the engagement ring that Jack picked out for me on his own. We announced our formal engagement to close friends and family in early December. Due to the distance, I did not receive my ring until December 26. I was so excited as I had never had a ring picked out for me and presented in such a romantic way. He had such good taste!

As we began discussing our future together, neither of us wanted a long engagement. We both agreed we were too old for a long courtship. During this time, I was still acting as a guest host every 3rd Sunday, on Reverend Durgan's "Sweet Hour of Prayer" radio program. I knew we needed to make an announcement as I did not want to have our beautiful relationship to be fuel for the town gossips. I was so happy to have Jack back in my life that I had not considered the likely move I would have to make to Columbus and began feeling anxious again. However, God gave me peace on this issue. We announced our pending marriage and my move to Columbus to the world just a few weeks later when I invited Jack to be my guest on the radio program.

Before our announcement, I had told Jack that when I moved from New Jersey to Mullens to Beckley, I saw myself living the rest of my life surrounded by my family and friends in WV. I really did not want to move again. However, my feelings on the move did not last long.

God reminded me of his word back in August 2009 that I would be going to church with my husband, and I shared this with Jack. This reminder eased my fears. I also realized that Columbus was closer and a more comfortable drive than I thought. I could be home in three short hours if my family needed me. We decided that if everything came together as planned, and with the help of the Lord, we would be married in June of 2010, in just six short months.

After the engagement, my girls and I started planning for the wedding. Since I was a young girl,

I had always dreamed of getting married in a beautifully decorated church, dressed in white. But would that still be appropriate for a sixty-three-year-old who had two prior marriages? See, neither of my previous weddings were in a church, and I did not marry in white. I struggled with this until I heard from the Lord again. He explained to me that the purity of white is for his church, a sign of virtue and righteous living. I realized that man-made rules that are often manipulated and did not apply to me as a member of the body of Christ. I was free to marry in white as I had always dreamed. God truly wanted me to have every desire of my heart. I never felt so loved and cherished by my father as I did at that moment.

God began opening the doors I needed to plan my dream wedding. In Beckley, we only had two stores that sold nice gowns. Both were very expensive, but my budget was limited. So when I heard that a local church was selling wedding gowns and prom dresses as a fundraiser to help young ladies who could not afford expensive gowns for prom, I knew I had to check it out. My sister, Thelma, my daughter, Melissa, and I went to the sale. On arrival, we went our separate ways hoping to better our chances of finding the special gown. I had come across several, but one, in particular, stood out to me. The church had done an excellent job of setting up dressing rooms to try on the gowns and even had large full-length mirrors you find in most high-end boutiques. I hesitated to try the dress, though it was my favorite, as it was slightly off the shoulder and exposed more than I was used showing. When I came out to see myself in the full-length mirror, I was unprepared for the applause and compliments that I received. This was such a fun experience. God blessed me to find the perfect "white" wedding gown I had so desired.

Jack and I were married on June 12, 2010, in Beckley, WV, by Pastor Sandra Jackson from The Word of Truth Church (COGIC). I joined The Word of Truth Church a few years after Jim passed, and I finished my tour of local churches in the area. Pastor Jackson, my family, and the church family helped me plan and experience my dream wedding. My wedding colors were pink, ivory and plum. My daughters were my maids of honor, and my friend Leola was my matron of honor. Our grand and great-granddaughters acted as flower girls.

Jack's son, Jackie Jr., was best man, and my two sons-in-law were groomsmen. My brother, Samuel, gave me away. Our grandson and great-grandson rolled out the carpet. Jack's son, Jermaine, was the pianist, and a dear friend of Jack's from Charlotte, NC, Stan Davis, sang the Lord's Prayer.

Jack's childhood friend, Donna Stallings, came in from Columbus to coordinate the wedding. Her daughter and my granddaughter were our ushers. My niece, Cassandra, traveled from Tampa, Florida, to help with my make-up and hair. My sisters, Thelma, and Carol (Pinky), eagerly helped with any last-minute issues that arose. Last but not least, our sweet niece, Renae (Madea), acted as doorkeeper for the bridal party as we got dressed at the church.

During the ceremony, Jack serenaded me with the song, "It's Your Time." While I knew Jack was a talented singer and planned to sing, the experience of having him sing "to me" after a lifetime apart was truly like a fairytale come true. I look back at the pictures and still cannot believe that God allowed me to have the wedding I had dreamed about as a young girl. But the greatest gift, that was totally unforeseen was that my first love would also be my last and final love. We honeymooned in Myrtle Beach, SC, and I relocated to Columbus, OH, shortly after that to begin a new and wonderful journey with my beloved.

7

MARITAL BLISS - MEET THE SMITHS

"BE COMPLETELY HUMBLE AND GENTLE; BE PATIENT, BEARING WITH ONE ANOTHER IN LOVE. MAKE EVERY EFFORT TO KEEP THE UNITY OF THE SPIRIT THROUGH THE BOND OF PEACE."
EPHESIANS 4:2-3

Oh, the things that Jack and I have shared. He is truly my gallant gentleman, not allowing me to put gas in my car, carry luggage, or unload groceries. It took a while to convince him that I could even open my own car door and did not need to sit and wait for him to open it for me.

I never imagined having a husband that would enjoy buying me clothes and purses to the point that I had to tell him to stop as I ran out of closet space. I have had to stop commenting on things I like, or need, as it was not long before they would show up in the house. I feel so blessed to have this wonderful man who feels nothing is too good for his wife.

We can be watching television together, and I can feel him watching me. When I look over, he is just smiling at me so sweetly. This used to make me uncomfortable as I was not used to this type of affection. Now, I appreciate knowing beyond a shadow of a doubt that he adores me and thinks I am beautiful.

Let me give you a bit more about Jack's background. He was a native of Eckman, WV, and his family later moved to Itmann, WV, where they remained until their move to Columbus, OH in 1960. Jackie was the youngest son of Deacon Lawrence and Evangelist Susie Smith. He graduated in 1962 from Linden McKinley High School and later went into the Army, serving his country from 1965-1967.

Shortly after returning home, he was blessed with his first child, Jacqueline. Jack, committed to his church and family, felt God's call on his life to do more for his kingdom. He met and married his sweetheart, Permelia Bailey. They had two sons, Jackie Jr., and Jermaine. Permelia was Jack's perfect match as she was also a gifted musician, singer, and songwriter.

As a family, the opportunity arose for them to join Keith Dobbins and the Resurrection Mass Choir, an internationally renowned recording artist. They recorded several albums, toured the world, including London, England, and appeared on the Bobby Jones Gospel television show in TN.

In addition to his music ministry, Jack also worked for Lucent Technologies for 33 years until his retirement. Jack passed his talent on to his sons, who are also accomplished musicians. They both play the keyboard, organ, drums, and bass guitar. Jack also taught numerous family and church members to play musical instruments through the years.

Jack is also an accomplished, self-trained photographer. Documenting life is one of his great passions, and his camera is never far from his grasp. Be it church services, conferences, weddings, or funerals - Jack has received requests to photograph them all. And he loves sharing his work via CD or DVD with anyone that asks. He keeps meticulous records, which has allowed him to provide photos of long passed family members, friends, and church members that mean so much to those that have lost them.

Jackie has been an active and devoted member of the Original Glorious Church of God in Christ, Columbus, OH, for over fifty years and is an ordained Elder. He retired as Minister of Music in 2016 after more than 5 decades of service in this position.

Upon moving to Columbus, I did not know how I would feel about joining Jack's home church. I was unfamiliar with the denomination and loved my former church in West Virginia. However, it was not long before I saw precisely why Jack was so devoted to the Original Glorious Church. I then remembered God's word to me, which had been fulfilled in less than one year. I was indeed going to church with my Husband and enjoying serving God with his people as I continue to grow in his word.

Jack's immediate family resides in Columbus, OH. In addition to his three children, he has 8 grandchildren and 14 great-grandchildren, along with a host of extended relatives and close family friends. While I have a few cousins and extended family members in Columbus, my children are in Texas.

Jack has been very supportive of me visiting my girls as often as possible. Melissa married a wonderful man of God in 2015 and moved to Arlington, TX. Moncherie and her family moved to Texas in 2007 and live in Highland Village, TX. We try to visit at least twice a year and look forward to relaxing and spending this precious time with them, as well as my four grandchildren and 1 great-grandson.

We travel extensively, which includes church conventions, family reunions, personal vacations, and overnight getaways, just because. I so enjoy meeting Jack's family at various reunions and family gatherings each year. So far, we have attended reunions in Newark, NJ, Danville, VA, Baltimore, MD, and Bluefield, WV. Our life together has been incredible.

Jack celebrated his seventy-fifth birthday on December 30, 2018, which was an extraordinary occasion. We planned his big event at the Berwick Party House. We had one hundred and fifty of his closest family members and friends there to help us celebrate his milestone birthday. The decorations were professionally done by TC^2 Services in his favorite black and gold motif. It was quite the gala affair, which was the highlight of our year.

8

JACK'S ATTACK

"NO WEAPON THAT IS FORMED AGAINST THEE
SHALL PROSPER; AND EVERY TONGUE THAT SHALL
RISE AGAINST THEE IN JUDGMENT THOU SHALT
CONDEMN. ISAIAH 54:17

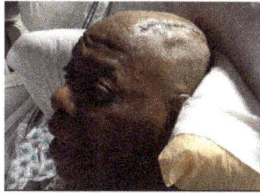

In January of 2019, my beloved found himself under attack. As true believers, we know that God's people are always targets of the enemy who seeks to kill, steal, and destroy our lives if we allow it.

My husband is a very healthy and active man. After retiring from Lucent, he took a few years off and found that he had too much time on his hands. He loves to drive and travel, so when an opportunity arose to drive for a leading bus company for Seniors, he was right on board. This led to him later becoming a school bus driver as he loves children and the schedule it afforded him.

Jack has always been mentally sharp and very quick-witted. He loves technology and gadgets and is constantly learning something new. I have come to depend on him so much, and I am very blessed that he enjoys pampering me.

So, when I noticed that he began slowing down a bit, dropping things, and searching a bit harder for words to finish a sentence, I was concerned. I would ask if he was okay, but he would always assure me that he was fine. I told you previously that he has played the keyboard and sang all of his life, so when he started forgetting the words to songs he had sung for decades, I knew something was not right. I wasn't sure if he was hiding an illness from me purposely so I would not worry, or if he genuinely didn't realize that something was terribly wrong.

Jack's memory issues persisted, so I began to insist that he at least speak to his oldest son, Jack Jr., about what was going on, but he refused. The Saturday morning before President's Day, we finally discussed my concerns, and he agreed to go to the doctor on Monday. It was a holiday, and he did not have to work. My spirit was troubled as I felt that Monday was just too far away, but I had to honor his decision and was happy that he had finally agreed to go.

That night a severe snowstorm hit the area, and the weather was treacherous. Most churches canceled Sunday services, so we slept in and were home when the electricity suddenly went off. We checked with our neighbors, most of whom were NOT affected. When we called the power company, we were told we were one of only five homes in our neighborhood to lose power. So, it might take a while for them to get out as they had more significant power outages all over the city.

After several hours, the temperature began to drop in the house, so we called Jack Jr. as he lived reasonably close to us. He immediately invited us over until our power was restored. While this might sound odd, I was so thankful for this storm as it provided the opportunity for Jack to discuss his memory issues with his son.

On arrival at Jack Jr.'s, we discussed the terrible weather, then fell into silence as we watched the news. It became apparent that Jack was not going to share his health concerns with his son. I told Jack Jr. that his dad had something to discuss with him. At first, Jack pretended he was watching television and did not hear me. Finally, Jack Jr. asked him what I was talking about.

When Jack turned to answer his son, he was speaking slowly. He was obviously having a difficult time finding the words to answer him. So, I spoke up, sharing my concerns with his dad's memory and behavior over the past few weeks. Jack Jr. was very upset that his father had not shared something so important with him. Jack Jr. and Marla, his wife, took over as I had prayed, they would. Within minutes we were all bundled up and on our way to the hospital, despite the weather.

WHEN WE ARRIVED at the emergency room, it was almost empty. Jack completed the registration process, and they took him back immediately to begin testing. As they explained, his symptoms were indicating a possible stroke. Jack had his first CT scan within the hour, and in less than thirty minutes, two doctors came in to talk with us concerning their findings.

They explained that it was not a stroke as initially suspected. However, they did find a small spot on his brain, indicating dried blood from a possible injury. They explained the location of the dried blood was applying pressure to his brain, which was likely causing his symptoms. They wanted to know if he had hit his head, fallen, or done anything resulting in a direct impact to his head. Jack could remember nothing of the sort. They recommended surgery as soon as possible, and he was scheduled for the next morning.

Jack does not care for hospitals, doctors, or needles. As he was always healthy, this was my first time seeing him in this environment, and my heart went out to him. He was very quiet, obviously uncomfortable with not being in control as he was so accustomed. Still, I have to say that he never once complained or questioned God or the situation. He told the Doctors to do what they had to do but just asked that they not share with him what the procedure would entail. Jack went into surgery at 7:30 am Monday morning.

Word spread quickly, and the next morning, Jacqueline and Jermaine joined Jackie Jr., Marla, and I at the hospital. Our Pastor, Dr. Bernita Wright, also came to lend moral and spiritual support as we waited for the surgery to end. Just the thought of brain surgery makes most of us shudder with fear. Through God's grace and mercy, Jack's surgery was over in less than forty-five minutes. His doctors found an old bleed, with a fresh bleed on top, which was the cause of his current symptoms. We learned later that the survival rate after an intracranial hemorrhage or brain bleed is very low, specifically for an African American male of Jack's age. He was in ICU for three days and was released only 4 days after his surgery. He made a full recovery in just two months with no residual loss of memory, speech, or motor skills.

Can I say here how awesome God is?!?! He used a snowstorm, which usually brings everything to stop, to "start" the process of getting my husband to the hospital. Then, on arrival at the ER, it was nearly empty. When does that ever happen? The fact that the doctor that read the CT scan was indeed an experienced brain surgeon, and we did not have to wait for one to be called in. Also, the fact that his schedule was free, and he was able to proceed the very next morning with Jack's surgery. This was all God's Handiwork. And finally, the fact that Jack made a full recovery with "no" long term or lingering issues is truly miraculous. Can you please join me in a Holy Shabach - a loud hallelujah giving praise to our Lord and Savior for my husband's life? Satan had no right to his life!

After 50 years apart and only 8 years of marriage, I was not allowing this attack to be more than just that, an "attempt" on his life. The power of prayer is real, and I admonish all women to listen to that still, small voice, that nagging feeling that refuses to go away. Because our God does still speak to us, and if we listen, we can avert many unforeseen tragedies in the lives of those we love.

9

MY ATTACK

"YOU RESTORED ME TO HEALTH AND LET ME LIVE.
SURELY IT WAS FOR MY BENEFIT THAT I SUFFERED
SUCH ANGUISH. IN YOUR LOVE YOU KEPT ME
FROM THE PIT OF DESTRUCTION" ISAIAH 38:16-17

After Jack's attack and miraculous full recovery, life went back to normal. Jack went back to work, and we had taken several weekend trips, including attending Jack's family reunion in Bluefield, WV. His family was so happy to see him doing so well after such a traumatic ordeal.

In early August, we decided we would go to our annual national church convention in Detroit, Michigan. I waited to get my hair done until the day before our departure, so it would be freshly done and hopefully last for the trip. I remember the date well; it was August 22, 2019. All went well, it is amazing how a little color and time with a stylist can make you feel so good. I was on my way back home when I was involved in a terrible car accident.

I have no doubt that my Guardian Angels were with me. I had taken my eyes off the road for only a moment as my water bottle rolled onto the floorboard. When I looked back up, the car in front of me had come to a complete stop. I swerved to avoid a direct rear impact with the vehicle in front of me, but I did not see the third car to my left and ended up hitting them both.

This was my first "at fault" accident after almost 50 years of driving. I was horrified and confused as to how it happened. I was not sure how I hit my head as my airbags deployed all around me. I was a little fuzzy, so I stayed in the car until two good Samaritans came and helped me out.

They took me to the side of the road and brought me a chair to sit down in. I was holding my head the entire time due to pain I couldn't explain. So, one of them went in search of an EMT. The police and ambulance had arrived, but they were checking on the others involved in the accident. I was so relieved to hear that no one else was hurt. After being checked, the technician put me in a cervical collar, and I was strapped to a gurney. I did not fully understand their urgency or why all of this was necessary. I was immediately taken to Mt. Carmel East Hospital in Columbus.

On arrival at the emergency room, everything became a blur. I was taken directly to a trauma unit where Xray and CT scans were obtained. They cut my clothes off to get me in a gown as they did not want to move my head, neck, or shoulders.

Once the shock wore off, I began having excruciating pain like I had never experienced in my life. I was admitted to ICU and given a strong sedative. I have little memory until I awoke the next morning with my dear husband by my side.

The doctor had already given Jack an update on the results of my tests, and I was shocked to hear that the Xray confirmed three fractures. I sustained a (C2) cervical spine fracture, a (T9-T10) thoracic spine fracture, and a rib fracture. They kept me medicated, and I was grateful for the relief and the comfort of having my sweet Jack and other family members by my side.

My oldest daughter, Melissa, who lives in Arlington, TX, was actually in Louisville, KY, that weekend to speak at a church youth conference. This was her first speaking engagement of this kind, and I was so proud of her. I knew she was anxious, so I asked Jack not to call her about the accident until after she spoke to prevent further stress or worry.

When Jack called with the news, Melissa did not hesitate. She called her husband in Texas to update him on the situation, and he agreed that she cancel her flight home the next day to proceed to Columbus to check on me. Vanessa, Melissa's friend, immediately canceled her flight home and rented her a car to get to Columbus, which was only a few hours away.

Melissa was at my bedside for almost two weeks. I was in ICU for 4 days until my doctor decided against surgical intervention. He was a leading trauma surgeon and was amazed that I was capable of movement and was not experiencing any paralysis. He expressed his concern about performing a spinal surgery due to my age. He advised that since I was doing so well and did not have impaired movement, he wanted to give my body a chance to heal on its own before revisiting his next steps.

I was in the hospital for a total of six days. I was then transferred to the Ohio Health Rehabilitation Center for an additional five days. I received

Physical Therapy and instruction on how to care for myself in the cervical brace that I was required to wear without causing further damage. Everyone I encountered was truly amazing and took excellent care of me.

The neurosurgeon, who opted to hold off on the surgery despite the contrary opinions of his peers, was a gift directly from God. I was in a cervical collar for almost five months. I was initially only allowed to remove the collar for showers. After nearly four months, I only had to wear the collar when riding in a car or at night while sleeping for support when I was not conscious of my movements.

I was finally released from wearing the cervical collar all together on January 16, 2020. My doctor was amazed at my recovery. He explained that he had doubts as to whether my spine would heal as it should due to my age. He was so pleased with my recovery and assured me that he had made the right decision. I know that God influenced his decision not to do the surgery, whether he was aware of it or not.

Today, I only have minor stiffness and pain when I do a bit too much. I can do everything I did before. I just had to learn to slow down and listen to my body. I still love to garden and tend to my roses, though I often must wait for my husband to leave the house before going out to work in the yard. I am so proud of my greens and tomatoes, and my roses are the envy of the neighborhood.

I am indeed one happy woman of God, and I know I received a modern-day miracle from my Heavenly Father. Throughout my hospitalization and recovery, numerous medical professionals told me how lucky I was to have survived such an injury. Still, Jack and I have always replaced "lucky" with "blessed" and let them know that God was my healer.

At my last appointment with the neurosurgeon, he again commented on how strong and lucky I was. As he explained, most seniors that sustain spinal injuries usually do not survive and that those that do rarely recover as quickly or as fully as I did. No one can ever tell me that I am not a beloved child of God!!!

My daughter, Melissa, my son, Jackie, and my wonderful husband took excellent care of me. My youngest daughter, Moncherie, wanted to be here, but she had just started a new job, so she called every day for an update. My missionary sisters came to see me, and I know the prayer warriors from my church bombarded heaven on my behalf. My pastor, Dr. Bernita Wright, was there with me as she was with Jack earlier in the year. I would be remiss if I did not mention my beautiful friend and neighbor, Barbara, who sent such sweet notes and gifts. I received so many flowers, cards, and goodies. I was honored and blessed as I did not realize how much I was loved.

With my attack, Satan tried a second time to beat the Smith's and end the union that God blessed, but our Lord is faithful, and his attempt on my life was unsuccessful. God has been good to me! I am so thankful for his love, his protection, his healing, and his mercy. But I am also grateful for the friends and family that supported Jack and I throughout the trying year of 2019.

10

LOVE, FAITH, AND PRAYER

"AND NOW THESE THREE REMAIN: FAITH, HOPE
AND LOVE. BUT THE GREATEST OF THESE IS LOVE."
1 CORINTHIANS 13:13

My goal in writing this book is to encourage women of all ages, especially those between sixty and eighty, to never give up on love with the help of God. Sometimes it takes a lifetime to find love or let it find you. For love is based on the scripture:

> *1 Corinthians 13:4, "Charity suffereth*
> *long, and is kind; charity envieth*
> *not; charity vaunteth not itself, is*
> *not puffed up,"*

Some women have learned from their mistakes, trying to find love on their own without the help of God. A Godly woman must include God in all her plans. Proverbs 3:5-6 tells us, "Trust in the Lord with all thine heart; and lean not unto thine own understanding. In all thy ways acknowledge him, and he shall direct thy paths."

Another scripture that comes to mind is Isaiah 40:31. We all must learn to "Wait upon the Lord" to renew our strength from all trials, loneliness, and everything in life that so easily besets us. We must learn to be patient in our waiting regardless of our age, as God knows the desires of our hearts.

I have friends and family that feel my situation is unique as they have been alone for so long, they have given up on love. Let me be clear that Jack and I are not receiving favoritism from God. The Word tells us that we are all blessed and highly favored when we are his children. God can give anyone the desires of their heart if they are open and willing to hear from and follow him. Make no mistake, neither of us are perfect, and our journey together has not been all peaches and cream.

Coming together after two prior marriages each, and half a century of outside influences, adult children, and so many other things did not result in an immediate "happily ever after." We were not discouraged because we knew marriage takes work. I believe that because of our experiences, both positive and negative, we were better prepared to work through any issues that arose. We respect one another's differences and know to quickly kiss and makeup after any disagreement, as not to give Satan entry into our warm and peaceful home.

At our age, we also have more time to spend together. I encourage Jack, who has far more energy than I do, to still be his own person. He pursues his hobbies and has maintained some of his regular routine that preceded me.

We as women need to be confident in the love of our spouse and encourage them as much as possible. When we become clingy and try to control or "influence" a grown man's every action, we are stifling our mates. But we are also limiting our own individuality and growth. Do not become a stumbling block in your own home over petty issues. As the word tells us, "It is better to live in a corner of the housetop [on the flat roof, exposed to the weather] Than in a house shared with a quarrelsome (contentious) woman." Proverbs 25:24 AMP

So, I encourage all women to trust God as he tells us in Jeremiah 29:11, that he plans for us to prosper if we would only trust him and get out of the way.

Ladies, we must spend more time in prayer. We must realize that God knows us better than we know ourselves. When we learn to keep our eyes on him, he can work on our behalf because he does genuinely want the very best for us. We must also walk in faith. Hebrews 11:1 tells us that "Faith is the substance of things hoped for and the evidence of things not seen." Allow my story to bolster your faith because what he did for me, he can also do for you. It is never too late for love.

ABOUT THE AUTHOR

Pamela Smith is first a Woman of God, Minister, Wife, Mother, and Grandmother. In addition to spending time with her family, she enjoys working in her garden, sewing, crocheting, and guiding and instructing young women on how to be Godly in this misguided world.